Contents

Introduction   2
APP level grids   5

Task 1	**A Tiny Treasure Hunt**	Teacher sheet	8
		Pupil sheet	9
		Assessment grid	10
Task 2	**Poorly Plants**	Teacher sheet	11
		Pupil sheet	12
		Assessment grid	13
Task 3	**Slime Olympics**	Teacher sheet	14
		Pupil sheet	15
		Assessment grid	16
Task 4	**Bright Bridges**	Teacher sheet	17
		Pupil sheet	18
		Assessment grid	19
Task 5	**Push Pals**	Teacher sheet	20
		Pupil sheet	21
		Assessment grid	22
Task 6	**Safe and Sound**	Teacher sheet	23
		Pupil sheet	24
		Assessment grid	25
Task 7	**Balls Galore**	Teacher sheet	26
		Pupil sheet	27
		Assessment grid	28
Task 8	**Heads Up**	Teacher sheet	30
		Pupil sheet	31
		Assessment grid	32
Task 9	**Counting Caterpillars**	Teacher sheet	33
		Pupil sheet	34
		Assessment grid	35
Task 10	**Sticky Fingers**	Teacher sheet	36
		Pupil sheet	37
		Assessment grid	38
Task 11	**Chocolate Choices**	Teacher sheet	39
		Pupil sheet	40
		Assessment grid	41
Task 12	**Marble Madness**	Teacher sheet	42
		Pupil sheet	43
		Assessment grid	44
Task 13	**Scilly Electricity**	Teacher sheet	45
		Pupil sheet	46
		Assessment grid	47
Task 14	**Lovely Bubbly**	Teacher sheet	48
		Pupil sheet	49
		Assessment grid	50

Introduction

APP for Science is designed to help you accurately assess your pupils' abilities using practical and research-based activities that are easy to use, understand and resource and which are fun for children to do. There is full curriculum coverage and support for ensuring skills progression.

What is Assessing Pupils' Progress for Primary Science (APP)?

APP is the new structured approach to teacher assessment, developed by the QCA in partnership with the DCFS, which helps teachers to make judgements on pupils' progress in Primary Science. It equips teachers with the tools to fine-tune their understanding of learners' needs and to tailor their planning and teaching accordingly. The aim is to provide a generalised agreement of pupil progress across the Primary phase to ensure skills progression into Key Stage 3.

APP is intended to be used as a periodic assessment of pupils through evidence collected of their work both written and otherwise.

The Assessment Foci

Pupils are assessed against five Assessment Foci (AFs). These are:

AF1: Thinking Scientifically. This focus involves children asking questions and understanding how science can answer such questions.

AF2: Understanding the Applications and Implications of Science. This focus looks at how children see science being used in their daily lives and draws on links between Science and Technology.

AF3: Communicating and Collaborating in Science. This focus concentrates on how children present their ideas about science, use scientific language and work together in a scientific context.

AF4: Using Investigative Approaches. This focus is on planning and doing investigations, collecting data and controlling risk.

AF5: Working Critically with Evidence. This focus concentrates on the thinking children have done in their investigations, what they found out and whether it was what they expected.

The benefits of APP

• Works together with Assessment for Learning strategies to help you learn more about pupils' strengths and weaknesses in science

• Helps you track pupil progress in science over time

• Allows you to make judgements about pupils' attainment linked to National Curriculum levels

• Provides a framework for you to share with pupils where they are and what they need to do to make progress

• Helps you in your curriculum planning and promotes teaching that is matched to pupil needs

• Helps you identify gaps in provision or areas that need review.

How to use this book

This book is intended to help you familiarise yourself with assessing the level of your pupils' work in real-life classroom practice in Primary Science. It is a book full of great ideas for investigations, and guidance notes and pointers on how children's responses to these investigations can inform your APP judgement.

APP Assessment Grid

At the beginning of this book we have provided a copy of the APP Assessment Foci Grid for Primary Science which comes from the DCSF. This assessment grid is designed to be photocopied and then highlighted so that following an assessment task you can level a child's work against each AF to see where they are at and what they need to do next to move up a level. It can then be used in subsequent assessment tasks to help you plot a child's progress and inform your future planning.

Tasks

There are 14 tasks which cover Key Stage 1 and are applicable to children in Year 1 and Year 2. We have linked task coverage to the National Curriculum Programme of Study and also to the QCA Scheme of Work. However, each task can stand alone and there are also opportunities which are broad ranging and aimed at giving children the opportunity to conduct full investigations which are not directly linked to the QCA Scheme of Work. There are two of these longer investigations per book.

Teacher Sheets

Each task incorporates a Teacher Sheet offering an overview of the task, detailing resources needed, the key concepts it covers and giving advice and support for undertaking it. There are also suggestions for ways of approaching the tasks and on outcomes and recording which can be adapted by you to suit the needs of your class. Throughout the course of the 14 tasks you will have the opportunity to revisit each Assessment Focus several times and to focus on different statements within the AF more than once. We outlined two main Assessment Foci for the standard tasks and there are two tasks which cover all five of the AFs.

Pupil Sheets

Each task also incorporates a Pupil Sheet to put the task in a fun and motivational context, prompt children as they undertake the task and outline key vocabulary.

Assessment Sheets

We have taken the larger APP Assessment Foci Grid and broken it down into more specific Assessment Grids which are relevant to the tasks within the book. As each task covers two AFs we have adapted the Assessment Grids for these AFs and given specific examples of what a child might say or do to help you make level judgements more easily. These grids are also designed to be photocopied and highlighted and, where appropriate, examples of the child's work attached as evidence. This can be kept as part of an assessment portfolio.

We have made suggestions as to which AF you might like to focus on for each investigation but this is not obligatory. If we have suggested that a particular task is suitable for assessing 'planning' for example, but you feel you'd rather concentrate on 'drawing conclusions', then that's fine. The tasks are quite open ended and the focus can be easily changed. The grids cover National Curriculum Attainment Levels 1, 2 and 3 in all the Assessment Foci (AF1–AF5).

Using the Tasks

The tasks are linked in to the most widely used science topic areas of the National Curriculum in Key Stage 1. The majority of tasks are suitable for use near the end of a topic when children have acquired some knowledge of the topic content and they can all be integrated into your own school's science planning. NB: We expect that you will make an assessment of your children's learning before starting any of the tasks and adapt them accordingly so opportunities for class and group discussions are included. Children should not feel as if they are being 'tested' by these tasks, it is the intention that the tasks can be incorporated into your normal planning for science.

The tasks cover at least three levels (1–3) in at least two AFs. This does not mean that you have to assess every statement in those levels for the task, only those you choose to focus on.

The tasks are designed to be completed within a morning or afternoon session although those tasks which involve observing and measuring over time (growing plants for example) will take longer.

You'll notice too that the tasks also provide opportunities to record or develop skills in literacy and mathematics and can be used as assessment opportunities for APP in those subjects too.

Working out a Level

We have designed the tasks to be teacher assessed as APP is a tool for teachers rather than a self review tool for children. However, you may wish to share Success Criteria with the children and we have given guidance on question prompts and discussion points within the teacher pages.

Within the task-specific assessment grids, we have provided level descriptors and detailed level progression across three levels for each of the featured AFs. Instead of only giving generalised statements, we have also provided examples of how certain statements can be demonstrated. NB: Due to the open nature of APP there will be more than one way of demonstrating each statement.

When a pupil satisfies the criteria for a particular level statement within a particular Assessment Focus, it provides evidence that the child is working at that level. The child does not need to satisfy all of the AF statements at that level to qualify as working securely within it.

Over Key Stage 1, children will produce a lot of work that can be assessed using the APP criteria and if a child is consistently satisfying statements within a particular level then that provides you with evidence that the pupil is working securely at this level.

Three reviews per year are recommended, and by incorporating some or all of these fourteen fun and engaging tasks into your science planning you will have a multitude of sound, reliable and realistic opportunities for assessing pupil's progress in science.

APP Primary Science Assessment Guidelines: Levels 1 and 2

	AF1 – Thinking scientifically	AF2 – Understanding the applications and implications of science	AF3 – Communicating and collaborating in science	AF4 – Using investigative approaches	AF5 – Working critically with evidence
L1	**Across a range of contexts and practical situations pupils:** • Ask questions stimulated by their exploration of their world • Recognise basic features of objects, living things or events • Draw on their everyday experience to help answer questions • Respond to suggestions to identify some evidence (in the form of information, observations or measurements) that has been used to answer a question	**Across a range of contexts and practical situations pupils:** • Identify a link to science in familiar objects or contexts • Recognise scientific and technological developments that help us	**Across a range of contexts and practical situations pupils:** • Use everyday terms to describe simple features or actions of objects, living things or events they observe • Present evidence they have collected in simple templates provided for them • Communicate simple features or components of objects, living things or events they have observed in appropriate forms • Share their own ideas with others and listen to the ideas of others	**Across a range of contexts and practical situations pupils:** • Respond to prompts by making some simple suggestions about how to find an answer or make observations • Use their senses and simple equipment to make observations	**Across a range of contexts and practical situations pupils:** • Respond to prompts to say what happened • Say what has changed when observing objects, living things or events
L2	**Across a range of contexts and practical situations pupils:** • Draw on their observations and ideas to offer answers to questions • Make comparisons between basic features or components of objects, living things or events • Sort and group objects, living things or events on the basis of what they have observed • Respond to suggestions to identify some evidence (in the form of information, observations or measurements) needed to answer a question	**Across a range of contexts and practical situations pupils:** • Express personal feelings or opinions about scientific or technological phenomena • Describe, in familiar contexts, how science helps people do things • Identify people who use science to help others • Identify scientific or technological phenomena and say whether or not they are helpful	**Across a range of contexts and practical situations pupils:** • Present their ideas and evidence in appropriate ways • Respond to prompts by using simple texts and electronic media to find information • Use simple scientific vocabulary to describe their ideas and observations • Work together on an experiment or investigation and recognise contributions made by others	**Across a range of contexts and practical situations pupils:** • Make some suggestions about how to find things out or how to collect data to answer a question or idea they are investigating • Identify things to measure or observe that are relevant to the question or idea they are investigating • Correctly use equipment provided to make observations and measurements • Make measurements, using standard or non-standard units as appropriate	**Across a range of contexts and practical situations pupils:** • Say what happened in their experiment or investigation • Say whether what happened was what they expected, acknowledging any unexpected outcomes • Respond to prompts to suggest different ways they could have done things
BL					
IE					

Overall assessment (tick one box only)   Low 1 ☐   Secure 1 ☐   High 1 ☐   Low 2 ☐   Secure 2 ☐   High 2 ☐   BL = 'Below Level'   IE = 'Insufficient Evidence'

Reproduced under the terms of the Click-Use Licence

APP Primary Science Assessment Guidelines: levels 3 and 4

	AF1 – Thinking scientifically	AF2 – Understanding the applications and implications of science	AF3 – Communicating and collaborating in science	AF4 – Using investigative approaches	AF5 – Working critically with evidence
L3	Across a range of contexts and practical situations pupils: • Identify differences, similarities or changes related to simple scientific ideas, processes or phenomena • Respond to ideas given to them to answer questions or suggest solutions to problems • Represent things in the real world using simple physical models • Use straightforward scientific evidence to answer questions, or to support their findings	Across a range of contexts and practical situations pupils: • Explain the purposes of a variety of scientific or technological developments • Link applications to specific characteristics or properties • Identify aspects of our lives, or of the work that people do, which are based on scientific ideas	Across a range of contexts and practical situations pupils: • Present simple scientific data in more than one way, including tables and bar charts • Use scientific forms of language when communicating simple scientific ideas, processes or phenomena • Identify simple advantages of working together on experiments or investigations	Across a range of contexts and practical situations pupils: • Identify one or more control variables in investigations from those provided • Select equipment or information sources from those provided to address a question or idea under investigation • Make some accurate observations or whole number measurements relevant to questions or ideas under investigation • Recognise obvious risks when prompted	Across a range of contexts and practical situations pupils: • Identify straightforward patterns in observations or in data presented in various formats, including tables, pie and bar charts • Describe what they have found out in experiments or investigations, linking cause and effect • Suggest improvements to their working methods
L4	Across a range of contexts and practical situations pupils: • Use scientific ideas when describing simple processes or phenomena • Use simple models to describe scientific ideas • Identify scientific evidence that is being used to support or refute ideas or arguments	Across a range of contexts and practical situations pupils: • Describe some simple positive and negative consequences of scientific and technological developments • Recognise applications of specific scientific ideas • Identify aspects of science used within particular jobs or roles	Across a range of contexts and practical situations pupils: • Select appropriate ways of presenting scientific data • Use appropriate scientific forms of language to communicate scientific ideas, processes or phenomena • Use scientific and mathematical conventions when communicating information or ideas	Across a range of contexts and practical situations pupils: • Decide when it is appropriate to carry out fair tests in investigations • Select appropriate equipment or information sources to address specific questions or ideas under investigation • Make sets of observations or measurements, identifying the ranges and intervals used • Identify possible risks to themselves and others	Across a range of contexts and practical situations pupils: • Identify patterns in data presented in various formats, including line graphs • Draw straightforward conclusions from data presented in various formats • Identify scientific evidence they have used in drawing conclusions • Suggest improvements to their working methods, giving reasons
BL					
IE					

Overall assessment (tick one box only) Low 3 ☐ Secure 3 ☐ High 3 ☐ Low 4 ☐ Secure 4 ☐ High 4 ☐ BL = 'Below Level' IE = 'Insufficient Evidence'

APP Primary Science Assessment Guidelines: levels 5 and 6

	AF1 – Thinking scientifically	AF2 – Understanding the applications and implications of science	AF3 – Communicating and collaborating in science	AF4 – Using investigative approaches	AF5 – Working critically with evidence
L5	**Across a range of contexts and practical situations pupils:** • Use abstract ideas or models or more than one step when describing processes or phenomena • Explain processes or phenomena, suggest solutions to problems or answer questions by drawing on abstract ideas or models • Recognise scientific questions that do not yet have definitive answers • Identify the use of evidence and creative thinking by scientists in the development of scientific ideas	**Across a range of contexts and practical situations pupils:** • Describe different viewpoints a range of people may have about scientific or technological developments • Indicate how scientific or technological developments may affect different groups of people in different ways • Identify ethical or moral issues linked to scientific or technological developments • Link applications of science or technology to their underpinning scientific ideas	**Across a range of contexts and practical situations pupils:** • Distinguish between opinion and scientific evidence in contexts related to science, and use evidence rather than opinion to support or challenge scientific arguments • Decide on the most appropriate formats to present sets of scientific data, such as using line graphs for continuous variables • Use appropriate scientific and mathematical conventions and terminology to communicate abstract ideas • Suggest how collaborative approaches to specific experiments or investigations may improve the evidence collected	**Across a range of contexts and practical situations pupils:** • Recognise significant variables in investigations, selecting the most suitable to investigate • Explain why particular pieces of equipment or information sources are appropriate for the questions or ideas under investigation • Repeat sets of observations or measurements where appropriate, selecting suitable ranges and intervals • Make, and act on, suggestions to control obvious risks to themselves and others	**Across a range of contexts and practical situations pupils:** • Interpret data in a variety of formats, recognising obvious inconsistencies • Provide straightforward explanations for differences in repeated observations or measurements • Draw valid conclusions that utilise more than one piece of supporting evidence, including numerical data and line graphs • Evaluate the effectiveness of their working methods, making practical suggestions for improving them
L6	**Across a range of contexts and practical situations pupils:** • Use abstract ideas or models or multiple factors when explaining processes or phenomena • Identify the strengths and weaknesses of particular models • Describe some scientific evidence that supports or refutes particular ideas or arguments, including those in development • Explain how new scientific evidence is discussed and interpreted by the scientific community and how this may lead to changes in scientific ideas	**Across a range of contexts and practical situations pupils:** • Describe how different decisions on the uses of scientific and technological developments may be made in different economic, social or cultural contexts • Explain how societies are affected by particular scientific applications or ideas • Describe how particular scientific or technological developments have provided evidence to help scientists pose and answer further questions • Describe how aspects of science are applied in particular jobs or roles	**Across a range of contexts and practical situations pupils:** • Identify lack of balance in the presentation of information or evidence • Choose forms to communicate qualitative or quantitative data appropriate to the data and the purpose of the communication • Distinguish between data and information from primary sources, secondary sources and simulations, and present them in the most appropriate form	**Across a range of contexts and practical situations pupils:** • Apply scientific knowledge and understanding in the planning of investigations, identifying significant variables and recognising which are independent and which are dependent • Justify their choices of data collection method and proposed number of observations and measurements • Collect data choosing appropriate ranges, numbers and values for measurements and observations • Independently recognise a range of familiar risks and take action to control them	**Across a range of contexts and practical situations pupils:** • Suggest reasons based on scientific knowledge and understanding for any limitations or inconsistencies in evidence collected • Select and manipulate data and information and use them to contribute to conclusions • Draw conclusions that are consistent with the evidence they have collected and explain them using scientific knowledge and understanding • Make valid comments on the quality of their data
BL					
IE					

Overall assessment (tick one box only)   Low 5 ☐   Secure 5 ☐   High 5 ☐   Low 6 ☐   Secure 6 ☐   High 6 ☐   BL = 'Below Level'   IE = 'Insufficient Evidence'

Task 1 — A Tiny Treasure Hunt

Teacher Sheet

APP	National Curriculum Programme of Study: Sc1 2b,e,f,h,j Sc2 1a Sc2 2g
AF1	Sc3 1a,b,c
AF3	QCA Scheme of Work: 1a

Task overview
An outdoor, classification exercise. Children collect objects based on teacher-selected criteria.

Key concepts
- Grouping and sorting
- Explain reasons for groupings
- Matching

Outcomes
- Children guess which criteria their partner used to make their collection.
- They explain why they chose the items they did.
- Whole class display of objects with reasons.

Resources
- large empty matchboxes
- depending on ability of children a colour, picture or word that can be described using the senses stuck into the inside base of the box e.g. 'spiky' or 'smooth' or a picture of a leaf or twig
- Task 1 Pupil Sheets

Teaching notes

- Set the scene for the task by explaining to children that we are going on a treasure hunt outside.

- Use a prepared large match box and open it to show children an image of something smooth like a pebble. Ask children what other things are smooth that they might put in the box. Write a collection of ideas on the board asking children for reasons for their choices.

- Tell children that it's very important that they keep what is inside their box a secret for now. Ask them to open their box and to look at the image or word without showing anyone.

- Explain that we are going to go outside and that they will have 15 minutes to find as many objects that are like their word or image as possible. The only rules are that they have to fit inside the match box and they must not be a living creature!

- Revise class rules for the outside with children, particularly what not to touch, e.g. mushrooms and berries.

- When the 15 minutes are up, bring children indoors and pair them. Each child takes it in turns to take out their 'treasure' and show their partner. The partner tries to guess what the image or word is. The child doing the showing then explains to their partner why they picked the objects. Together children decide if all the objects are suitable.

- Make a display of the matchboxes with accompanying explanations.

- Extend to cover things that were once alive or never alive.

Task 1 A Tiny Treasure Hunt

We're going on a treasure hunt!

What you need to do
- Collect things that match the word or picture in your matchbox.
- Show your partner what you collected.
- Can they guess what word or picture was in your matchbox?

You may find these words helpful
the same, like, similar, feels like, looks like, shape

Task 1 — A Tiny Treasure Hunt

Assessment Sheet

	Level 1 Across a range of contexts and practical situations pupils:	Level 2 Across a range of contexts and practical situations pupils:	Level 3 Across a range of contexts and practical situations pupils:
AF1 Thinking scientifically	• Respond to suggestions to identify some evidence (in the form of information, observations or measurements) that has been used to answer a question e.g. *All the objects are green so that must have been the word.* • Recognise basic features of objects, living things or events e.g. **can pick objects from a given selection that match their picture or word**	• Draw on their observations and ideas to offer answers to questions e.g. *The leaf is green but the glass is not. I think they are all smooth objects.* • Make comparisons between simple features or components of objects, living things or events e.g. *I picked these because they are all spiky.*	• Identify differences, similarities or changes related to simple scientific ideas, processes or phenomena e.g. **can identify objects that were once the same but are no longer similar, such as leaf plucked from a tree and leaf found on floor; can describe similarities and differences** • Use straightforward scientific evidence to answer questions, or to support their findings e.g. *When I touch the objects they feel spiky. This was the word used in the box.*
AF3 Communicating and collaborating in science	• Use everyday terms to describe simple features or actions of objects, living things or events they observe e.g. *This is green and smooth.* • Share their own ideas with others and listen to the ideas of others e.g. **can give a reason why they picked the objects**	• Use simple scientific vocabulary to describe their ideas and observations e.g. *These are all different kinds of leaf.* • Work together on an experiment or investigation and recognise contributions made by others e.g. *Kai used these ones because they were green.*	• Use scientific forms of language when communicating simple scientific ideas, processes or phenomena e.g. **can use scientific language to describe the difference between a living leaf and a dead leaf** • Identify simple advantages of working together on experiments or investigations e.g. *When we worked together we could find more things that matched.*

© Pearson Education Ltd 2010. APP for Science Years 1 and 2

Teacher Sheet

Task 2 Poorly Plants

| APP
AF4
AF5 | **National Curriculum Programme of Study:** Sc1 1 2e,f,h,i   Sc2 3a
QCA Scheme of Work: 1b |

Task overview
Investigate conditions for healthy growth in plants.

Key concepts
- Observing and describing
- Comparing
- Measuring
- Observing over time

Outcomes
- Children write instructions for how to keep plants healthy.

Resources
- selection of broad bean seedlings or other fast growing plants – make sure they are a few weeks old
- multi-link or other non-standard measure or strips of paper that children cut to size
- rulers if children able to read scale
- graduated beaker or large and small containers to measure out water
- Task 2 Pupil Sheets

Teaching notes

- Set the scene for the task by explaining that Mr Davis is a teacher and he likes growing plants in his classroom. However, when he comes into work one morning he discovers the plants on his desk are not looking very well.

- What do children think has gone wrong? *Why are the plants growing outside doing well? What do they have that the indoor ones don't?* (water from rain, sunlight)

- Explain that you've been growing some plants at home. *Maybe we could use these to do a test to see what helps plants grow well.*

- Ask children what they think they should test (light conditions or amount of water) or split the groups and do both investigations. Help children to plan their investigation and decide what they will be doing.

- Encourage them to look very carefully at the healthy plants. Can they describe them? *How tall are they? How many leaves do they have?*

- With children put some plants in a sunny place, some in a shady place and some in the dark and water them with the same amount of water. Measure the plants regularly and count the leaves.

- Put some plants in a sunny place and give one third lots of water every day, one third a little water every day and remainder no water. Measure the plants regularly and count the leaves over a few weeks.

- As well as recording changes in height (in non-standard or standard units depending on the child) and number of leaves, what other changes do the children notice?

- Using the evidence from their investigations, children write some instructions for Mr Davis advising him what to do to keep his plants healthy indoors.

Task 2 Poorly Plants

Mr Davis likes growing plants.

Can you help him?

What you need to do
- Talk to your partner about what plants need to grow well and what Mr Davis forgot to do.
- Write a 'to do list' to help Mr Davis remember.

You may find these words helpful
light, dark, water, grow, die, fair test, plant

Assessment Sheet

Task 2 Poorly Plants

	Level 1 Across a range of contexts and practical situations pupils:	Level 2 Across a range of contexts and practical situations pupils:	Level 3 Across a range of contexts and practical situations pupils:
AF4 Using investigative approaches	• Respond to prompts by making some simple suggestions about how to find an answer or make observations e.g. **We could put some plants in the dark.** • Use their senses and simple equipment to make observations e.g. **These leaves are yellow.**	• Identify things to measure or observe that are relevant to the question or idea they are investigating e.g. **We can measure how tall the plants grow.** • Make measurements using standard or non-standard units as appropriate e.g. **This plant is 5 blocks high.**	• Identify one or more control variables in investigations from those provided e.g. **We need to water the plants at the same time every day.** • Make some accurate observations or whole number measurements relevant to questions or ideas under investigation e.g. **measures plant height in centimetres**
AF5 Working critically with evidence	• Respond to prompts to say what happened e.g. **The plant on the windowsill was the biggest.** • Say what has changed when observing objects, living things or events e.g. notices changes in shape, colour or texture of leaves and differences between plants kept in good and poor conditions	• Say what happened in their experiment or investigation e.g. **We found the plant we gave the middle amount of water to grew the tallest.** • Say whether what happened was what they expected, and acknowledging any unexpected outcomes e.g. **I thought the plant we watered most would grow best but it almost died!**	• Identify straightforward patterns in observations or in data presented in various formats, including tables, pie and bar charts e.g. **can refer to changes in height represented on a bar chart** • Describe what they have found out in experiments or investigations, linking cause and effect e.g. **knows that volume of water given is important to plant growth but that too much is as detrimental as too little**

© Pearson Education Ltd 2010. APP for Science Years 1 and 2

Task 3 Slime Olympics

Teacher Sheet

APP	National Curriculum Programme
AF3	of Study: Sc1 1 Sc1 2f,g Sc3 1a
AF4	QCA Scheme of Work: 1c

Task overview

Children investigate how far different slimes travel. They make measurements and record them.

Key concepts
- Recognise similarities and difference
- Make accurate measurements
- Record results

Outcomes
- Children measure how far different slimes travel down a slope.
- They record the results in a table, chart and/or graph

Resources
- up to four different slimes including commercially produced slimes and/or cornflour slime made by mixing cornflour and water in differing amounts (aim to have slimes that are different in appearance and texture)
- A3 tray or whiteboard
- non standard measures e.g. Lego or multi-link
- standard measure e.g. cm tape measure
- 10-second timer e.g. sand timer, water timer, tocker or simple (second only) stop watch
- pre-prepared two column table for children to record measurements (headings: type of slime /how far it went)
- 1st, 2nd, 3rd, 4th stickers
- squared paper
- Task 3 Pupil Sheets

Teaching notes

- It may be useful to have children work in maths ability groups for this activity.

- Give children time to freely explore a range of different slimes. Ask them to describe the slimes by asking them about the similarities and differences. Get them to talk about how they look, feel and smell. Do they have one they like best? Why is it their favourite? Get the children to give a name to each of the different slimes. Try to encourage funny names such as Gooey Godfrey or Slimy Sue.

- Set the scene for the task by explaining that we are going to have a Slime Olympics. The first event is to see which slime slides/travels furthest down a slope in 10 seconds. They will be able to think of some other events later.

- *Which slime do you think will win the first event? Why?*

- Show children how to put the slime on a cross drawn at the top of the tray or whiteboard and then gently lift the tray or board up to create a slope. Explain that they keep the tray lifted for 10 seconds. Demonstrate how the 10-second timers work.

- Children work in groups of four. They take it turns to lift the board, watch the timer for 10 seconds, measure how far the slime has travelled using standard or non-standard measurements according to ability and record the results.

- Have a pre-prepared table for children that might find constructing their own table too challenging. You may also like to provide order stickers (1st, 2nd, 3rd, 4th) for children who can not yet make measurements.

- Once the table is completed with results, children make individual charts or simple graphs on squared paper.

Task 3 Slime Olympics

How far can slime slide in 10 seconds?

Can you find out?

What you need to do
- Talk to your team. Which slime do you think will win? Why?
- Test each slime.
- Write down how far they go in a chart.
- Which slime won the gold medal?

You may find these words helpful
slime, thick, sticky, timer, measure, far, furthest, fair, run, test

Task 3 Slime Olympics

Assessment Sheet

	Level 1 Across a range of contexts and practical situations pupils:	Level 2 Across a range of contexts and practical situations pupils:	Level 3 Across a range of contexts and practical situations pupils:
AF3 Communicating and collaborating in science	• Present evidence they have collected in simple templates provided for them **e.g. puts order (1st, 2nd, 3rd, 4th) stickers on a table next to the slimes** • Communicate simple features or components of objects, living things and events they have observed in appropriate forms **e.g. talks about slimes sliding down the slope**	• Present their ideas and evidence in appropriate ways **e.g. records results in a table of how far the slimes stretched** • Use simple scientific vocabulary to describe their ideas and observations **e.g. talks about the slime that stretched the furthest and their idea why**	• Present simple scientific data in more than one way, including tables and bar charts **e.g. records results in a table and produces a bar chart showing the distances the slimes stretched** • Use scientific forms of language when communicating simple scientific ideas, processes or phenomena **e.g. talks about gravity pulling the slimes down the slope or possibly the role of the different levels of viscosity the slimes seem to have**
AF4 Using investigative approaches	• Respond to prompts by making some simple suggestions about how to find an answer or make observations **e.g. suggests lifting the card higher if the slimes don't start to stretch very much** • Use their senses and simple equipment to make observations **e.g. observes the order of how far the slimes stretch**	• Correctly use equipment provided to make observations and measurements **e.g. uses blocks to measure length of slime stretch and tocker or sand/water timer to time 10 second interval** • Make measurements using standard or non-standard units as appropriate **e.g. measures slime stretch in Lego blocks or multi-link cubes**	• Select equipment or information sources from those provided to address a question or idea under investigation **e.g. chooses a stop watch and a ruler to measure 10 seconds time and the length of slime stretch** • Make some accurate observations or whole number measurements relevant to questions or ideas under investigation **e.g. measures slime stretch in cms using ruler or tape measure**

16 © Pearson Education Ltd 2010. APP for Science Years 1 and 2

Teacher Sheet

Task 4 Bright Badges

APP	National Curriculum Programme of Study: Sc1 1 Sc1 2b,c,e,f,g,j Sc3 1a–d Sc4 3b
AF2	
AF3	QCA Scheme of Work: 1d

Task overview
Children investigate which materials show up best in dim light conditions.

Key concepts
- Light and dark
- Reflection
- Useful applications of science knowledge
- Fair test

Outcomes
- Children make reflective badges.
- They explain why they have chosen the materials they have.

Resources
- pictures of people wearing high visibility clothing working outside in heavy traffic
- high visibility jacket
- 8 cm² card (1 per child)
- glue (suitable to stick fabric and paper to card)
- large safety pins
- sticky tape
- scissors
- selection of different coloured fabrics and papers including silver, gold and fluorescent orange, pink and yellow
- dark room, table and thick blanket to make a dark den or dark box made out of a shoe box
- torch
- Task 4 Pupil Sheets

Teaching notes

- Set the scene for the task by asking children whether they can see as well in the dark as the daytime. Ask them what they could wear to keep safe when they are outside in the dark or dusk.

- Wear the high visibility jacket and display the pictures of traffic workers. Ask children why they are wearing them. Can they think of anybody else who wears them?

- Show children a selection of different coloured fabrics and papers. Ask them to tell a partner which ones they think would be easy to see in dim light and which ones wouldn't.

- Explain that they are going to design and make a badge to help them be seen by the traffic when it is dark. Tell them that they must choose the best materials to do this. Encourage them to test the materials, e.g. they can take the material into a cupboard with a low powered torch instead of having the light on or they can put a bit of the material at the end of a dark box and look through a small hole at the other end.

- Explain you want them to be able to tell the other children why they have made their choice of materials.

- Demonstrate how to attach the safety pin to one side of the card using tape and how to cut and stick a piece of material to the other using the glue. Tell the children they can choose more than one type of material to make their badge and make different designs.

- Test the badges in a darkened room. Allow them to compare how effective their badges are in the dark. Use a torch as car head lights and point it at some of the badges to illustrate how useful their badges are at helping them to be seen by the driver.

Pupil Sheet

Task 4 Bright Badges

Which colours show up best in dim light?

Can you find out?

What you need to do
- Test the materials to find out which ones show up best in dim light.
- Share your ideas with the other children on your table.
- Make a badge to wear that will help drivers spot you when it is getting dark.

You may find these words helpful
dim, light, bright, shiny, dull, material, reflect

Assessment Sheet

Task 4 Bright Badges

	Level 1 Across a range of contexts and practical situations pupils:	Level 2 Across a range of contexts and practical situations pupils:	Level 3 Across a range of contexts and practical situations pupils:
AF2 Understanding the applications and implications of science	• Identify a link to science in familiar objects or contexts **e.g. knows that highly reflective materials can be seen at night** • Recognise scientific and technological developments that help us **e.g. says that high visibility clothing is good to wear if you are working near traffic**	• Describe, in familiar contexts, how science helps people to do things **e.g. says that high visibility clothing is good to wear if you are working near traffic because the drivers can see you** • Identify scientific or technological phenomena and say whether or not they are helpful **e.g. knows that having reflective bands on coats, shoes and bags can help cut down road accidents**	• Explain the purposes of a variety of scientific or technological developments **e.g. explains why highly reflective materials are used round traffic cones** • Link applications to specific characteristics or properties **e.g. can accurately predict which untested materials would be good to use in visibility jackets explaining why**
AF3 Communicating and collaborating in science	• Communicate simple features or components of objects, living things and events they have observed in appropriate forms **e.g. talks about some of the materials they have used on their badge saying they have chosen them because they show up well** • Share their own ideas with others and listen to the ideas of others **e.g. says which materials they think will not be any good to use in their badge and asks other children what they think**	• Use simple scientific vocabulary to describe their ideas and observations **e.g. talks about materials that are easy to see in dim light (shiny, bright and/or fluorescent) being best to use on their badge** • Work together on an experiment or investigation and recognise contributions made by others **e.g. thanks another pupil for suggesting trying the silver paper**	• Use scientific forms of language when communicating simple scientific ideas, processes or phenomena **e.g. talks about why reflective materials are suitable to use on their badge** • Identify simple advantages of working together on experiments or investigations **e.g. comments on it being easier to test the materials working with a partner as one could hold the torch as the other swopped the different materials being tested and they can discuss which are good at reflecting**

© Pearson Education Ltd 2010. APP for Science Years 1 and 2

Task 5 Push Pals

Teacher Sheet

APP	National Curriculum Programme of Study: Sc1 1 Sc1 2a,b,f,g,h Sc4 2b
AF1	QCA Scheme of Work: 1e
AF3	

Task overview

Children explore a range of 'push down spring up' toys. They make comparisons and decide which they believe works best and can say why.

Key concepts
- Pushes are forces
- Making observations
- Working together

Outcomes
- Children write an advertising postcard for a springy toy explaining why the toy they have chosen works best.

Resources
- collection of different push down toys (the type with vertical visible springs that have suckers so they stick down briefly before springing up)
- a blank postcard for each child
- meter ruler
- timer (seconds)
- writing and drawing equipment
- Task 5 Pupil Sheets

Teaching notes

- Show the children a collection of different 'push down spring up' toys. Ask a child to choose one. Demonstrate how the toy works. Ask children to describe to another child sitting close to them what happened.

- Ask another child to choose a second toy. Ask children to talk to their neighbour what they think will happen when you push down this second toy. Encourage children to describe what was similar and different about how the toys worked.

- You might want to demonstrate both toys again. Ask them questions about the way they spring up. *Which toy took longest to spring up?* (Can children count in seconds?) *Which jumped highest or straightest?* Estimate using meter rule.

- Set the scene for the task by explaining that Mrs Spring owns a toy shop and these toys have not sold very well even though they are only £1 each. Some of them have been returned by customers. In future, she will only sell the ones that work well so would like children to find this out for her.

- Tell children they are going to find out which one they think works best. When they have decided they must make a post card advertising the toy in Mrs Spring's toy shop window. The advert must have a picture of the one they have chosen. They can also write down why they made their choice on the card.

- Explain that they are going to work in groups to explore the toys but they can choose any one of the toys for their favourite. They can choose the same or different ones.

Task 5 Push Pals

Mrs Spring owns a toy shop.

Help Mrs Spring find out.

What you need to do
- Try out some of the 'springy' toys.
- In groups find out which toy works best.
- Write an advert for Mrs Spring's window saying which is the best and why.

You may find these words helpful
push, down, jump, spring, up, fast, high, time, count

Assessment Sheet

Task 5 Push Pals

	Level 1 Across a range of contexts and practical situations pupils:	Level 2 Across a range of contexts and practical situations pupils:	Level 3 Across a range of contexts and practical situations pupils:
AF1 Thinking scientifically	• Respond to suggestions to identify some evidence (in the form of information, observations, measurements) that has been used to answer a question **e.g. We can see which one jumps highest.** • Ask questions stimulated by their exploration of their world **e.g. wonders which toy will jump highest?**	• Draw on their observations and ideas to offer answers to questions **e.g. The size of push doesn't seem to make a difference to the height the toy reaches it always bounces up about the same height.** • Make comparisons between basic features or components of objects, living things or events **e.g. states the rabbit toy pops up quicker than the monster**	• Identify differences, similarities or changes related to simple scientific ideas, processes or phenomena **e.g. has realised the toys with the bigger springs jump higher** • Use straightforward scientific evidence to answer questions, or to support their findings **e.g. The thicker the metal the spring is made out of the higher the toy jumps.**
AF3 Communicating and collaborating in science	• Use everyday terms to describe simple features or actions of objects, living things or events they observe **e.g. The toy jumps up.** • Communicate simple features or components of objects, living things and events they have observed in appropriate forms **e.g. produces a postcard showing a good jumping toy**	• Use simple scientific vocabulary to describe their ideas and observations **e.g. When I push down hard the toy takes longer to jump up.** • Work together on an experiment or investigation and recognise contributions made by others **e.g. knows if they all let go of toys together they can see which toy jumps up quickest**	• Use scientific forms of language when communicating simple scientific ideas, processes or phenomena **e.g. can communicate that when you push the toy down the suckers stick together but the squashed spring stretches back to its normal shape and size and forces the toy up** • Identify simple advantages of working together on experiments or investigations **e.g. realises that by working together we can test the toys quicker and make direct comparisons**

Teacher Sheet

Task 6 Safe and Sound

APP	National Curriculum Programme of Study: Sc1 1 Sc1 2b,f,g Sc3 1a–d
AF2	Sc4 3c,d
AF3	QCA Scheme of Work: 1f

Task overview

Children research ear protection and its importance in some jobs. They investigate best material for sound insulation.

Key concepts
- Sound
- Collect evidence
- Test materials
- Science and technology have useful applications in everyday life.

Outcomes
- Children perform a short drama piece that demonstrates why ear protection is important.
- They make some ear protectors.

Resources
- books, pictures and ICT resources showing people wearing ear protectors to reduce sound levels
- pairs of ear protectors (if possible)
- samples of good sound insulating materials
- camcorder to record plays
- Task 6 Pupil Sheets

Teaching notes

- Ask children if they know how we hear things. Talk to them about how wonderful it is to be able to hear. Get them to close their eyes and listen for a minute. What can they hear?

- Ask them to cover their ears with their hands and listen again. *What is the difference?*

- Ask children a range of questions about loud sounds e.g. *When have you heard loud noises? What things can you think of that make loud sounds? What is the loudest sound you can ever remember hearing? Are there any loud sounds you like? Are there any you don't like? How can we make them seem quieter? Can you think of people that have to work with lots of noise? What do they do to make it quieter for themselves?*

- Set the scene for the task by explaining that Sunil's dad works for the council digging up roads and he has to wear ear protectors. *Why does he have to do this?* Show children the ear protectors and/or pictures showing people wearing them in their work.

- Tell children they are going to use the books, pictures, CD ROMs etc to find out more about ear protection.

- Explain that they are going to test different insulating materials to find out which are the best to use to make some ear protectors.

- They then make up a short play about why ear protection is important, using the ear protectors they have made as a prop.

- When they have finished the plays encourage children to show their plays to each other. Record them if possible.

Task 6 Safe and Sound

Sunil's dad wears ear protection in his job.

Why does he wear ear protectors?

What you need to do

- Find out about other people who use ear protectors in their job. Why do they wear them?
- Test different materials to see if any would make good ear protectors.
- Make up a play with your group about keeping your hearing safe.

You may find these words helpful

ear, hearing, protect, protectors, loud, quiet, noise, hurt, muffle

Task 6 Safe and Sound

Assessment Sheet

	Level 1 Across a range of contexts and practical situations pupils:	Level 2 Across a range of contexts and practical situations pupils:	Level 3 Across a range of contexts and practical situations pupils:
AF2 Understanding the applications and implications of science	• Identify a link to science in familiar objects or contexts e.g. **Fluffy ear muffs keep our ears warm and they make it more difficult to hear.** • Recognise scientific and technological developments that help us e.g. **Ear protectors stop our hearing getting damaged.**	• Express personal feelings/opinions about scientific or technological phenomena e.g. **Ear protectors are good as without them we may go deaf.** • Identify scientific or technological phenomena and say whether or not they are helpful e.g. **Drills are great to break up the hard road quickly but make a lot of noise that can damage ears.**	• Explain the purposes of a variety of scientific or technological developments e.g. **Ear protectors have been designed to have insulating materials to stop loud sound entering our ears and damaging them.** • Identify aspects of our lives, or of the work that people do, which are based on scientific ideas e.g. **People may wear headphones in offices so that they can to listen to materials playing on their computers keeping it to themselves and not disturbing others and keeping out the office noise.**
AF3 Communicating and collaborating in science	• Use everyday terms to describe simple features or actions of objects, living things or events they observe e.g. **The fluffy material seemed to make everything go quiet.** • Present evidence they have collected in simple templates provided for them e.g. **picks thick material to make ear protectors for the drama sketch**	• Present their ideas and evidence in appropriate ways e.g. **demonstrates the use of ear protection as part of the piece of drama or dramatises damage to ears if not wearing protection** • Respond to prompts by using simple texts and electronic media to find information e.g. **finds an illustration and information about ear protection in a book or CD-ROM**	• Present simple scientific data in more than one way e.g. **displays understanding of sound insulation as part of the piece of drama** • Use scientific forms of language when communicating simple scientific ideas, processes or phenomena e.g. **talks about sound insulation when describing how the ear protectors work**

© Pearson Education Ltd 2010. APP for Science Years 1 and 2

Task 7 Balls Galore

Teacher Sheet

APP
AF1 AF2 AF3
AF4 AF5

National Curriculum Programme of Study: Sc1 1   Sc1 2a–j
Sc3 1a–d

Task overview
Children choose a question related to a property of balls to investigate. They plan, carry out and evaluate the investigation.

Key concepts
- Collecting evidence
- Making observations
- Making measurements
- Fair test

Outcomes
- Children formulate a suitable question about how balls behave.
- Plan and carry out an investigation.
- Make an appropriate record and evaluation.

Resources
- large collection of balls used for sport (different sizes, shapes, colours and materials)
- large strips of paper and marker pens
- simple cm marked tape measures
- lolly sticks, straws, garden canes etc to take simple uniform non standard measures /measurements
- balls of string or wool to help with comparative measures
- simple 1-second timer stopwatch/ stopclock/tocker
- paper and pencils
- Task 7 Pupil Sheets

Teaching notes

- Allow children some exploration time with the balls in the hall or outside.
- Ask them about the things they did and how the balls behaved. Did they try bouncing the balls? Rolling the balls? Catching the balls? Did they try more than one ball?
- Ask them to name games they know that involve a ball. *What does the ball need to do to be used in that game?* E.g. a ball must be bouncy to be used in basketball.
- Can they think of any people who make money playing with balls? *Why are they paid?*
- Set the scene for the task by explaining that professional sports people such as footballers need good quality balls to use.
- Tell children they are going to work in groups to find out something about the balls.
- Explain that you want to find out if it is easier to throw bigger balls. Choose three balls of different colours, shape and material. Ask children to discuss with a partner whether you have chosen the right three balls. Listen to see if some of them understand that you should have chosen balls of the same material and shape to make it a fair test.
- Tell the children that in their groups they must come up with a question they want to find out about. They must write it on a strip of paper and show it to you before they start their investigation. Check they have chosen a question which is easy to identify what they are changing e.g. material and what they are measuring e.g. height of bounce. Once you have checked their question explain they can only choose three balls and tell them they can choose their measuring equipment.
- They record their results and write down what they have found out about the balls. *Is this information useful for the sports people? Will it help them find the best ball?*

Pupil Sheet

Task 7 Balls Galore

These sports people need to play with the best balls.

Help them find out which balls are best.

What you need to do
- In your group, decide what you would like to find out about the balls. Write this as a question.
- Choose and test three balls that will help you find out the answer to your question.
- What did you find out? Write it down for the sports people.

You may find these words helpful
balls, measure, fair

© Pearson Education Ltd 2010. APP for Science Years 1 and 2

Task 7 Balls Galore

Assessment Sheet

	Level 1 Across a range of contexts and practical situations pupils:	Level 2 Across a range of contexts and practical situations pupils:	Level 3 Across a range of contexts and practical situations pupils:
AF1 Thinking scientifically	• Respond to suggestions to identify some evidence (in the form of information, observations, measurements) that has been used to answer a question e.g. *The best ball goes high.* • Ask questions stimulated by their exploration of their world e.g. *Do bigger balls bounce higher than smaller balls?*	• Draw on their observations and ideas to offer answers to questions e.g. *The plastic ball bounces more times.* • Respond to suggestions to identify some evidence (in the form of information, observations or measurements) needed to answer a question e.g. *The best ball will bounce highest.*	• Identify differences, similarities or changes related to simple scientific ideas, processes or phenomena e.g. *I think the material will affect how high the ball bounces.* • Respond to ideas given to them to answer questions or suggest solutions to problems e.g. *We can test how high each ball bounces.*
AF2 Understanding the applications and implications of science	• Identify a link to science in familiar objects or contexts e.g. *The bouncy ball is best.* • Recognise scientific and technological developments that help us e.g. *recognises that new and better balls might be made of materials that weren't invented long ago such as foam rubber or plastic*	• Express personal feelings or opinions about scientific or technological phenomena e.g. *This ball is best because it is nice and bouncy.* • Identify scientific or technological phenomena and say whether or not they are helpful e.g. *Having soft bouncy balls is nice because they don't sting you when you catch them.*	• Explain the purposes of a variety of scientific or technological developments e.g. *A leather ball is good to kick in a game of football because it is firm and goes a long way.* • Link applications to specific characteristics or properties e.g. *Basketballs need to be bouncier than footballs because they are dribbled in a different way.*
AF3 Communicating and collaborating in science	• Communicate simple features or components of objects, living things and events they have observed in appropriate forms e.g. *The ball bounced very high.* • Share their own ideas with others and listen to the ideas of others e.g. *says they should roll the balls down a ramp or says they think this is a good idea if someone else suggests it*	• Present their ideas and evidence in appropriate ways e.g. *can use a simple table to record results* • Work together on an experiment or investigation and recognise contributions made by others e.g. *children work together so one rolls the balls, another measures how far they went and another records the results*	• Present simple scientific data in more than one way, including tables and bar charts e.g. *produces a two column table showing material and number of bounces and produces a bar chart of these results* • Identify simple advantages of working together on experiments or investigations e.g. *Our group worked well because I dropped the ball and my friend could see how high it bounced.*

© Pearson Education Ltd 2010. APP for Science Years 1 and 2

Assessment Sheet

Task 7 Balls Galore

	Level 1 Across a range of contexts and practical situations pupils:	Level 2 Across a range of contexts and practical situations pupils:	Level 3 Across a range of contexts and practical situations pupils:
AF4 **Investigative approaches**	• Respond to prompts by making some simple suggestions about how to find an answer or make observations e.g. **We can see how high the ball bounces.** • Use their senses and simple equipment to make observations e.g. **cuts lengths of string to the distance the different sized balls roll and can say which rolled furthest**	• Identify things to measure or observe that are relevant to the question or idea they are investigating e.g. **We need to measure how high the ball bounces.** • Make measurements using standard or non-standard units as appropriate e.g. **can measure the height the balls bounce in lolly sticks**	• Identify one or more control variables in investigations from those provided e.g. **We need to drop the balls from the same height to make it a fair test.** • Make some accurate observations or whole number measurements relevant to questions or ideas under investigation e.g. **uses a stop watch to time how many seconds it takes a ball to stop bouncing or a tape measure to see how high it bounces**
AF5 **Working critically with evidence**	• Respond to prompts to say what happened e.g. **The rubber ball bounces more times.** • Say what has changed when observing objects, living things or events e.g. **child can say the balls will roll different distances**	• Say what happened in their experiment or investigation e.g. **The rubber ball bounced the highest height.** • Say whether what happened was what they expected, acknowledging any unexpected outcomes e.g. **I thought the rubber ball would bounce higher and it did.**	• Identify straightforward patterns in observations or in data presented in various formats, including tables, pie and bar charts e.g. **The harder balls bounced highest.** • Describe what they have found out in experiments or investigations, linking cause and effect e.g. **The rubber ball bounced higher because it is made from harder material than the sponge or plastic ball.**

© Pearson Education Ltd 2010. APP for Science Years 1 and 2

Task 8 Heads Up

Teacher Sheet

APP	National Curriculum Programme of Study: Sc1 1 Sc1 2b,h Sc2 2a Sc2 4a
AF1	QCA Scheme of Work: 2a
AF3	

Task overview
A measuring and comparing activity. Children identify that our heads do not grow as much as the rest of our bodies.

Key concepts
- Observe, recognise and compare
- We grow as we get older

Outcomes
- Children order pictures of people according to age.
- They draw a picture of what they think an adult would look like if heads grew at same rate as bodies.

Resources
- pictures/photographs of real babies, children of different ages and adults.
- visit from real baby (if possible)
- baby dolls and teenage dolls
- simple tape measure
- string
- long ribbon
- good quality large round balloons
- balloon pumps
- double sided sticky tape
- play dough (only for the extension activity)
- Task 8 Pupil Sheets

Teaching notes

- Set the scene for the task by explaining that a new born baby's head circumference is usually about half its length. Its head length is about a quarter of its length.

- Demonstrate measuring head circumference and length on a couple of children using a simple tape measure or using string. Give children chance to measure heads. What do they notice about the size? (all similar size) Blow a balloon up to the size of an average child's head.

- Choose a child to measure your head. What do they notice? (not much bigger) Now blow a balloon up to the size of your head.

- Measure a medium height child from shoulder to feet and ask one of them to measure you. What do they notice this time?

- Cut a ribbon to the shoulder of both the child and you. Measure the baby in the same way or say that you have measured a friend's baby and have a pre cut ribbon and balloon.

- Display the ribbons vertically with one end touching the floor. Stick the balloon heads on the top of each ribbon. Talk about how they are different.

- Give each group of children a selection of pictures showing babies, children and adults. Give them a baby doll and a teenage doll. Ask them to order the pictures baby to adult.

- Challenge them to draw a picture of what they think an adult would look like if their head grew at the same rate as their body. What size have they made the heads? Why did they choose the size they have?

- An extension to this activity they make play dough models of what they have drawn.

Pupil Sheet

Task 8 Heads Up

Do our heads grow as much as the rest of our bodies?

What you need to do
- Order pictures of people from youngest to oldest.
- Draw a picture of what you think an adult might look like if our heads grew as much as our bodies.

You may find these words helpful
head, length, measure, height, tall, big, bigger, small, smaller

Task 8 Heads Up

Assessment Sheet

	Level 1 Across a range of contexts and practical situations pupils:	Level 2 Across a range of contexts and practical situations pupils:	Level 3 Across a range of contexts and practical situations pupils:
AF1 **Thinking scientifically**	• Respond to suggestions to identify evidence (in the form of information, observations, measurements) that has been used to answer a question **e.g. looks at a picture of baby and an adult and says the baby's head looks bigger** • Ask questions stimulated by their exploration of their world **e.g. asks if some animal babies have heads that look bigger compared to their bodies than their parents (do puppies seem to have large heads)**	• Draw on their observations and ideas to offer answers to questions **e.g. refers to the display, dolls and/or pictures and states that heads don't grow in the same way as the rest of our bodies so as we get older they seem smaller in comparison** • Respond to suggestions to identify some evidence (in the form of information, observations, measurements) needed to answer a question **e.g. when asked what they would do to be sure will say they would measure heads**	• Represent things in the real world using simple physical models **e.g. blows up a balloon to represent an adult head if it had grown in the same way as the rest of their body** • Use straightforward scientific evidence to answer questions, or to support findings **e.g. talks about pictures/measurements showing how heads don't grow as much as other bits of bodies**
AF3 **Communicating and collaborating in science**	• Use everyday terms to describe simple features or actions of objects, living things or events they observe **e.g. can say we get bigger as we get older** • Communicate simple features or components of objects, living things and events they have observed in appropriate forms **e.g. talks about their head being similar size to the teacher's head**	• Respond to prompts by using simple texts and electronic media to find information **e.g. finds an appropriate illustration in a book or CD-ROM of people of different ages to compare appearance of relative head size** • Use simple scientific vocabulary to describe their ideas and observations **e.g. can talk about growth and heads not growing as much**	• Present simple scientific data in more than one way, including tables and bar charts **e.g. can predict to add to the ribbon and balloon display demonstrating understanding of the pattern of how head growth should relate to someone growing taller** • Use scientific forms of language when communicating simple scientific ideas, processes or phenomena **e.g. talks about heads growing proportionally less than the rest of our bodies as we get older**

© Pearson Education Ltd 2010. APP for Science Years 1 and 2

Teacher Sheet

Task 9 Counting Caterpillars

APP	National Curriculum Programme of Study: Sc1 2e–h,j Sc2 4b Sc2 5a–c
AF3	QCA Scheme of Work: 2b
AF5	

Task overview
An outdoor, pattern seeking activity where children hunt for woolly caterpillars and create tally chart.

Key concepts
- Recognising patterns
- Plants and animals in the environment
- Camouflage

Outcomes
- Children identify patterns in data.
- They translate tally chart to bar graph.

Resources
- A3 whiteboard or card (portrait) with strip of hooked Velcro stuck horizontally across the board at approximately 10 cm intervals
- woolly caterpillars made from 10 cm lengths of coloured wool:
  - 25 x bright yellow
  - 25 x red
  - 25 x dark green
  - 25 x brown
- timer
- copy of bar chart for children to complete
- Task 9 Pupil Sheets

Teaching notes

- Prepare the activity by placing the coloured lengths of wool around the school playground/garden. Make sure the various colours are evenly spread.
- Set the scene for the activity by explaining to children that we're going outside to hunt very special woolly caterpillars and we want to see how many we can find as quickly as possible. Talk about why we won't collect real caterpillars.
- Show the prepared board to which you have attached Velcro strips. Explain that each strip represents one minute of time.
- As children find the caterpillars they come and stick the wool on the appropriate Velcro strip forming a basic tally chart.
- Work in groups and let each group have one minute each (or longer depending on the conditions) knowing that the later groups will find fewer pieces of wool.
- Once all of the caterpillars have been found come back to the classroom and look at the recording board. Do children notice anything? (They found more caterpillars in the first minutes and fewer at the end; they found the brightly coloured ones first.)
- Talk about what the results tell us about caterpillars or other small animals in the school playground/garden. *Why might it be a good idea for the caterpillars to be the same colour as the plants or soil? Why do we need to take care of the small creatures in our environment?*
- Turn the board on its side and show children how it now resembles a bar chart. Children complete template of bar chart provided or construct their own depending on ability.

Task 9 **Counting Caterpillars**

Pupil Sheet

Hunt the woolly 'caterpillars'.

How easy are they to find?

What you need to do
- Hunt for the 'caterpillars'.
- Stick them on the board.
- Talk about what you notice.
- Draw a chart of your results.

You may find these words helpful
colour, hide, find, dark, light, more, most, fewest, number, minute

Task 9 — Counting Caterpillars

Assessment Sheet

	Level 1 Across a range of contexts and practical situations pupils:	Level 2 Across a range of contexts and practical situations pupils:	Level 3 Across a range of contexts and practical situations pupils:
AF3 Communicating and collaborating in science	• Present evidence they have collected in simple templates provided for them e.g. **can complete pictogram chart which is given to them to show number of caterpillars collected** • Share their own ideas with others and listen to the ideas of others e.g. **if working in groups can decide who takes the first turn to collect the caterpillars or where to look**	• Present their ideas and evidence in appropriate ways e.g. **can present information as a simple tally chart** • Work together on an experiment or investigation and recognise contributions made by others e.g. **Amy went first and looked in the bushes; I went next and looked in the grass.**	• Present simple scientific data in more than one way, including tables and bar charts e.g. **translates data from tally chart to bar chart** • Identify simple advantages of working together on experiments or investigations e.g. **We all helped so we collected the caterpillars really quickly and no one got too tired.**
AF5 Working critically with evidence	• Respond to prompts to say what happened e.g. **The yellow caterpillars were easy to find.** • Say what has changed when observing objects, living things or events e.g. **knows it's harder to find the caterpillars at the end of the activity**	• Say what happened in their experiment or investigation e.g. **We found the most caterpillars in the first three minutes.** • Say whether what happened was what they expected, acknowledging any unexpected outcomes e.g. **I thought we'd find all the yellow ones first but we didn't find them all.**	• Identify straightforward patterns in observations or in data presented in various formats, including tables, pie and bar charts e.g. **The chart shows we found more caterpillars at the beginning and most were brightly coloured. It was harder to find any at the end and they were mostly brown.** • Describe what they have found out in experiments or investigations, linking cause and effect e.g. **We found the brightly coloured caterpillars easily; the brown ones were more difficult to spot because they were camouflaged and didn't show up as easily.**

© Pearson Education Ltd 2010. APP for Science Years 1 and 2

Task 10 Sticky Fingers

Teacher Sheet

APP
AF1
AF5

National Curriculum Programme of Study: Sc1 1   Sc1 2b,g,h   Sc2 4a
QCA Scheme of Work: 2c

Task overview
Children carry out an investigation and construct a scatter graph to examine how their height relates to their reach. They use the graph to spot trends.

Key concepts
- Similarities and differences
- Recognise trends

Outcomes
- Children record findings.
- They draw what a person might look like if their finger print was in the top left hand side of the graph.

Resources
- large roll of plain paper (e.g. lining paper)
- fingerprint pad or paint on a sponge
- tape measure
- marker pen
- Blu-tack (plenty of it to hang paper)
- height chart
- strips of paper
- Post-it notes
- Task 10 Pupil Sheets

Teaching notes

- In preparation, hang four pieces of plain white wall paper next to each other from ceiling to floor. The graph will be constructed onto this. Draw on a horizontal and vertical axis using a thick marker pen. The horizontal axis is the height axis the vertical axis is the reach up the wall.

- Set the scene for the task by explaining to children that when you are at home it's always the tallest member of the family that gets the plates down from the top shelf because they are they are the only one who can reach them. This has made you curious to know if taller people can always reach higher.

- Ask children if they think this is true and ask them how we could find out? Show them the giant graph axis and explain that they are going to find out by constructing a graph so that they can see the results. Start with six children from your class. Ask children which six should be chosen. Encourage them to choose children who differ in height.

- Measure each child in turn and ask them to stand next to their height measurement on the horizontal axis. Get them to put fingerprint ink on their middle finger and reach up as high as they can and make a print at the limit of their reach. When you have six prints ask if they can spot a pattern. How could they improve the graph? *Would more children's prints help? Should we get some smaller and taller children from other classes to add to the data?*

- Collect six younger and then six older children from different classes and ask them to add their fingerprint to the graph. Encourage children to study the graph and working in pairs write something the graph tells them on a strip of paper. Discuss them with children and display them on the graph.

- Finally ask them to draw on Post-it notes what they think a child might look like if their finger print was in the top left and or the bottom right of the graph. Display.

Pupil Sheet

Task 10 Sticky Fingers

Can tall people always reach higher?

What you need to do

• With your partner look at the finger print graph. Write down one thing you notice about the graph.

• Draw a picture of what a person might look like if their fingerprint was in the top left hand side of the graph.

You may find these words helpful

height, tall, taller, short, shorter, reach, pattern, trend

Task 10 Sticky Fingers

Assessment Sheet

	Level 1 Across a range of contexts and practical situations pupils:	Level 2 Across a range of contexts and practical situations pupils:	Level 3 Across a range of contexts and practical situations pupils:
AF1 Thinking scientifically	• Respond to suggestions to identify some evidence (in the form of information, observations, measurements) that has been used to answer a question **e.g. Mathew is tall and he could reach really high.** • Ask questions stimulated by their exploration of their world **e.g. Can the tallest person reach the highest?**	• Draw on their observations and ideas to offer answers to questions **e.g. If children had put finger prints in the top right of the graph they would need to be short with long arms.** • Make comparisons between basic features or components of objects, living things or events **e.g. notices two children that were exactly the same height didn't have exactly the same reach**	• Respond to ideas given to them to answer questions or suggest solutions to problems **e.g. can explain how to carry out an additional investigation to see if the pattern is the same for boys and girls** • Use straightforward scientific evidence to answer questions, or to support their findings **e.g. The graph shows us that shorter children can't usually reach as high as taller children but this isn't always true.**
AF5 Working critically with evidence	• Respond to prompts to say what happened **e.g. All the reception children are short and they couldn't reach very high.** • Say what has changed when observing objects, living things or events **e.g. state that as we get older we get taller and can reach higher**	• Say what happened in their experiment or investigation **e.g. states that usually taller children could reach higher** • Say whether what happened was what they expected, acknowledging any unexpected outcomes **e.g. I thought the year 4 children would be able to reach higher because they are taller and most could but Sarah couldn't because she has shorter arms.**	• Identify straightforward patterns in observations or in data presented in various formats, including tables, pie and bar charts **e.g. Generally the taller you are the higher you can reach.** • Suggest improvements to their working methods **e.g. realises that if they used more people we would be more certain of the results**

38

© Pearson Education Ltd 2010. APP for Science Years 1 and 2

Teacher Sheet

Task 11 Chocolate Choices

APP	National Curriculum Programme of Study: Sc1 2a,b,c,g Sc3 2b
AF4	
AF5	QCA Scheme of Work: 2d

Task overview

Children plan and carry out an investigation to find the best chocolate to make chocolate buttons quickly. They record results on a recipe card.

Key concepts
- Materials change when heated and cooled
- Make predictions
- Review and improve method.

Outcomes
- Children prepare a recipe card showing how to make speedy chocolate buttons.

Resources
- suitable cups for hot drinks such as take away card coffee cups with plastic lids
- white cooking chocolate
- milk cooking chocolate
- dark cooking chocolate
- greaseproof paper
- lolly sticks or tea spoons
- hot (not boiling) water in flasks
- simple stop watches
- card
- writing and drawing equipment
- camcorder
- Task 11 Pupil Sheets

Teaching notes

- Bring in a selection of cup cakes with chocolate buttons for decoration. Take a button off the top of some of the cakes. Ask children what would happen if you heated them up. Put the buttons on greaseproof paper on the radiator or over a cup of hot water.

- **Safety note – water should be hot to touch but not hot enough to scald.**

- Set the scene for the task by explaining that Clare Cooper the owner of Clare's Cup Cake Emporium has so many orders for cup cakes that she needs to be able to make them quickly. All of Clare's cakes are handmade and all have her special heart-shaped chocolate button on the top. The problem Clare has is that the chocolate can take a long time to melt and even longer to set. Tell children that she wants them to find out which is the best type of chocolate to make speedy chocolate buttons.

- Check to see if the buttons that you left in a hot place have melted. Pass them round still on the greaseproof paper for the children to see. Ask them how they have changed.

- Ask a few children to try changing the shape of the melted button into a heart using a lolly stick or teaspoon. Ask how they can get the heart-shaped buttons to set quickly. If they suggest a fridge or freezer tell them there isn't one available. A cooler area of the classroom should be cool enough for the chocolate to solidify.

- Show children all the equipment available to them: cups with lids, different types of chocolate, hot water, lolly sticks, timers, greaseproof paper, etc. Before they start they must predict which will be the speediest chocolate to use and spot any risks. For example, hot water could burn them.

- Children test out the chocolate, take recordings to find out which is the best chocolate to use then produce a recipe card for Clare. Explain that they can change what they do if it doesn't work perfectly first time. They could also do a video demonstration if they prefer.

Task 11 Chocolate Choices

Pupil Sheet

Clare Cooper has a cake shop.

Help Clare find the best chocolate to make her hearts.

What you need to do
- Talk in groups to decide which chocolate you think will melt quickest.
- Melt and set each chocolate. Order the chocolate.
- Write your recipe on a card for Clare to use.

You may find these words helpful
melts, sets, solidifies, solid, liquid, chocolate, white, milk, dark

Task 11 Chocolate Choices

Assessment Sheet

	Level 1 Across a range of contexts and practical situations pupils:	Level 2 Across a range of contexts and practical situations pupils:	Level 3 Across a range of contexts and practical situations pupils:
AF4 **Using investigative approaches**	• Respond to prompts by making some simple suggestions about how to find an answer or make observations **e.g. suggests we could test the different types of chocolate by holding them in a warm hand to see if they go runny** • Use their senses and simple equipment to make observations **e.g. touches the chocolate to see how it is changing as it warms up**	• Identify things to measure or observe that are relevant to the question or idea they are investigating **e.g. observes which type of chocolate melts quickest and takes least time to set** • Make measurements using standard or non-standard units as appropriate **e.g. measures how long it takes for the chocolate to completely melt or completely set in using a sand or water timer**	• Make some accurate observations or whole number measurements relevant to questions or ideas under investigation **e.g. measures in minutes and seconds using a stopwatch or simple timer and can state which is the quickest melting and/or solidifying type of chocolate** • Recognise obvious risks when prompted **e.g. understands the water must only be hand hot not boiling as it can burn**
AF5 **Working critically with evidence**	• Say what has changed when observing objects, living things or events **e.g. comments on the chocolate going soft and runny** • Respond to prompts to say what happened **e.g. these may be inaccurate …says the chocolate might get bigger as it gets cooked; or more accurate… says the chocolate will go soft and runny**	• Say whether what happened was what they expected, acknowledging any unexpected outcomes **e.g. expresses surprise that they didn't all melt at the same rate and talks about the fact that they have different things in them that must change this** • Respond to prompts to suggest different ways they could have done things **e.g. says that putting them on the heat at the same time would have made it easier to see which melted fastest**	• Describe what they have found out in experiments or investigations, linking cause and effect **e.g. realises that not all types of chocolate melt and solidify at the same rate and talks about them having different ingredients** • Suggest improvements to their working methods **e.g. realises that weighing the pieces of chocolate and ensuring they were all the same mass would have made the test fairer**

© Pearson Education Ltd 2010. APP for Science Years 1 and 2

Teacher Sheet

Task 12 Marble Madness

APP	**National Curriculum Programme of Study:** Sc1 2b,d,e,f,g,h,i,j Sc4 2a,c
AF4	**QCA Scheme of Work:** 2e
AF5	

Task overview
Children investigate how to use a marble and a ramp to make a marble at the bottom of the ramp travel a distance.

Key concepts
- Know that when things move there is a cause
- Solve problems
- Describe findings

Outcomes
- Children demonstrate what they did in their investigation.
- They explain their decisions.
- They measure the distance the marble goes.

Resources
- marbles of various sizes and colours
- 6 cm x 100 cm lengths of card folded in half along their length to form channel for marbles to roll down
- metre rulers
- tape measures
- lolly sticks or other suitable uniform non-standard unit measuring equipment
- Task 12 Pupil Sheets

Teaching notes

- Set the scene for the task by explaining to children that when their grandparents or great grandparents were little there were no TVs or computers but some of the toys were the same. Show children how to play marbles and let them have a game in small groups.

- Once they have had chance to explore tell them that there are many more games that use marbles and that one of these is Marble Madness. To play this game they have to use a marble ramp and two marbles. One marble is placed at the bottom of the ramp and the other is rolled down the ramp into the waiting marble.

- The winner is the person who manages to knock their marble at the bottom of the ramp the furthest. Players are allowed to use any two marbles and alter the height of the ramp for the launch marble. The launch marble must always start at the top of the ramp. They are not allowed to push the marble down the ramp.

- Tell children they are going to work in groups to find how to get their ramp bottom marble to go furthest.

- When they have carried out their investigations let them demonstrate what they have done and ask them to measure the distance the marble travels. Question them about their method and the other things they discovered.

- Children could go on to invent marble games of their own.

Task 12 Marble Madness

Play Marble Madness.

"We have to make the bottom marble go a long way."

Can you help?

What you need to do
- Talk in your group about how you are going to make the bottom marble travel a long way.
- Show everyone what you did.

You may find these words helpful
marble, ramp, height, hit, far, close, roll

Task 12 Marble Madness

Assessment Sheet

	Level 1 Across a range of contexts and practical situations pupils:	Level 2 Across a range of contexts and practical situations pupils:	Level 3 Across a range of contexts and practical situations pupils:
AF4 **Using investigative approaches**	• Respond to prompts by making some simple suggestions about how to find an answer or make observations **e.g. suggests trying to roll the marble from different ramp heights high, medium and low and comparing how far the base marble travels** • Use their senses and simple equipment to make observations **e.g. can say which marble they saw go furthest**	• Make some suggestions about how to find things out or how to collect data to answer a question or idea they are investigating **e.g. suggests trying different ramp heights and measuring how far the base marble travels** • Correctly use equipment provided to make observations and measurements **e.g. uses equipment to make simple measurements of ramp height and distance travelled by the marble**	• Identify one or more control variables in investigations from those provided **e.g. states that they can only change the ramp height and must keep other things the same** • Make some accurate observations or whole number measurements relevant to questions or ideas under investigation **e.g. selects metre ruler to control ramp height and tape measure to measure how far the base marble travels**
AF5 **Working critically with evidence**	• Respond to prompts to say what happened **e.g. can say whether a high, mid or low ramp helped the base marble go further** • Say what has changed when observing objects, living things or events **e.g. notices that the marbles travel different distances when the ramps are at different heights**	• Say what happened in their experiment or investigation **e.g. reports what altering the ramp height did to the distance the marble travelled** • Say whether what happened was what they expected, acknowledging any unexpected outcomes **e.g. I thought the big marble would go furthest and I was right.**	• Identify straightforward patterns in observations or in data presented in various formats, including tables, pie and bar charts **e.g. spots that the higher the ramp the further the base marble travels up to a top ramp height of…** • Describe what they have found out in experiments or investigations, linking cause and effect **e.g. talks about higher ramps leading to the base marble moving further as the ramp marble hits it faster or harder**

Teacher Sheet

Task 13 Scilly Electricity

APP	National Curriculum Programme of Study: Sc1 2b Sc4 1a
AF2	QCA Scheme of Work: 2f
AF3	

Task overview
Discuss news story about Isles of Scilly E-day to discuss appliances which use electricity and ways to save electricity.

Key concepts
- Electricity generation
- Use of electrical appliances
- Energy conservation

Outcomes
- Children produce a poster showing ways to save electricity and why it is important not to waste electricity.

Resources
- UK map
- pictures of electrical and non-electrical appliances
- poster paper
- coloured pens
- Internet access
- Katie Morag stories
- Task 13 Pupil Sheets

Teaching notes

- Ask the children how many electrical appliances they used before coming to school today. How many other appliances in their home use electricity? Use pictures of appliances to sort into electrical and non-electrical.

- Set the scene for the activity by showing children a map and pointing out the Isles of Scilly (pronounced 'silly'). Introduce E-Day as a special day when the people who lived on the islands tried to save energy. If possible show children websites that covered the event: go to **www.pearsonhotlinks.co.uk**, search for APP for Science and click on this activity.

- Discuss what actually happened and why. Energy consumption had only gone down by 1.2%. The newspaper reported that one school had baked scones and that it was a cold, dark day. *Why might baking not help? Why might bad weather make it difficult to save energy?*

- Discuss ways in which electricity could be saved e.g. switching appliances off when they are not needed, doing a task by hand instead of by machine, having low energy, efficient appliances etc. Also discuss ways in which electricity could be wasted.

- *Where does electricity come from?* Discuss how most of our electricity is generated by power stations which use oil, coal or gas (fossil fuels) or nuclear fuel. *Why is it important that electricity is not wasted?*

- Children design a poster to advise how electricity should be used wisely and reasons why it should not be wasted.

- Discuss alternative energy sources: wind, tidal, water, sun, etc.

- Link life living on an island to the adventures of Katie Morag on the Island of Struay.

| Pupil Sheet |

Task 13 Scilly Electricity

The Scilly Isles had a special save energy day.

They didn't save much electricity! Can you help them?

What you need to do
- Make a poster showing the people of the Scilly Isles how to save electricity and why they shouldn't waste it.

You may find these words helpful
electricity, machines, heat, light, cost, waste, switch, save

Assessment Sheet

Task 13 Scilly Electricity

	Level 1 Across a range of contexts and practical situations pupils:	Level 2 Across a range of contexts and practical situations pupils:	Level 3 Across a range of contexts and practical situations pupils:
AF2 Understanding the applications and implications of science	• Identify a link to science in familiar objects or contexts e.g. *Electricity makes the washing machine go.* • Recognise scientific and technological developments that help us e.g. *Washing machines help us to wash clothes more easily.*	• Express personal feelings/opinions about scientific or technological phenomena e.g. *You shouldn't waste electricity.* • Describe in familiar contexts, how science helps people do things e.g. *Electricity can be very useful because a lot of machines do work to help us, for example, dishwashers.*	• Explain the purposes of a variety of scientific or technological developments e.g. *gives examples of how different appliances use electricity; Light bulbs use electricity to make light.* • Identify aspects of our lives, or of the work that people do, which are based on scientific ideas e.g. *Some lights are designed to use less energy than others.*
AF3 Communicating and collaborating in science	• Communicate simple features or components of objects, living things or events they have observed in appropriate forms e.g. *can group pictures of everyday appliances which do and do not use electricity in a simple two-set diagram* • Use everyday terms to describe simple features or actions of objects, living things or events they observe e.g. *knows that electricity is not being used when appliances are switched off*	• Respond to prompts by using simple texts and electronic media to find information e.g. *can use a website to find out about saving electricity* • Use simple scientific vocabulary to describe their ideas and observations e.g. *TVs need to be switched off to save electricity.*	• Present simple scientific data in more than one way, including tables and bar charts e.g. *can produce a poster which includes data about energy use* • Use scientific forms of language when communicating simple scientific ideas, processes or phenomena e.g. *Electricity can be used to make light, heat, sound and movement.*

© Pearson Education Ltd 2010. APP for Science Years 1 and 2

Teacher Sheet

Task 14 Lovely Bubbly

APP
AF1 AF2 AF3
AF4 AF5

National Curriculum Programme of Study: Sc1 1   Sc1 2 a–j
Sc3 1a   BoS 1a 2b

QCA Scheme of Work: n/a

Task overview
Children make bubble mixtures using different washing-up liquids. They compare bubble sizes.

Key concepts
- Fair test
- Making accurate measurements
- Making observations
- Getting results
- Evaluating evidence

Outcomes
- Children draw graph of results.
- They write a note to the twins explaining how they did the experiment and what they found out.

Resources
- different brands of washing-up liquids including 'economy' and 'luxury' option
- glycerine (available from chemists and supermarkets)
- water
- bubble blowers (commercially produced or pipe cleaners bent to shape)
- sheets of sugar paper/blotting paper
- cm ruler
- multi-link
- Task 14 Pupil Sheets

Teaching notes

- Set the scene for the task by explaining to children that you wanted to help the twins make bubble mixtures for their party but when you looked for a recipe all the washing-up liquids said that **they** were the best to use.

- Ask children if they can help find the best mixture to use.

- With children make up a bubble mixture using one of the brands: 2 tablespoons of washing-up liquid; 1 teaspoon of glycerine; 1 cup of water. Allow children time to practise blowing the biggest bubble they can. Explain that the best way to blow really big bubbles is to blow gently for a longer time rather than short bursts. When children are confident, they need to choose a child to blow a big bubble and then try to 'pop' it onto blotting paper.

- Repeat with the next brand of washing-up liquid. Discuss with children what needs to be kept the same to make it fair. *What are we changing (testing)?* Elicit that there needs to be the same amount of all the ingredients to make the test fair and only the brand of washing up liquid can change.

- When children have investigated all the different bubble mixtures and have blotting paper evidence discuss with children which of the washing-up liquids makes the biggest bubble. Use a centimetre ruler to measure the diameter of the circle or with less able children use multi-link.

- Children record results in a two column table then translate this to a bar chart with brand of washing-up liquid on the x-axis and diameter of bubble in cm on the y-axis.

- They write to the twins telling them which washing-up liquid to use and how they found out.

Task 14 Lovely Bubbly

The twins are having a party.

We want to make some big bubbles at our party.

What you need to do
- Test different bubble mixture. How big was your biggest bubble?
- Draw a graph of your results.
- Write to the twins telling them what you did and which mixture to use.

You may find these words helpful
bubble, blowing, bigger, smaller, mix, glycerine, washing up liquid, water, change, test

Task 14 Lovely Bubbly

Assessment Sheet

	Level 1 Across a range of contexts and practical situations pupils:	Level 2 Across a range of contexts and practical situations pupils:	Level 3 Across a range of contexts and practical situations pupils:
AF1 Thinking scientifically	• Respond to suggestions to identify some evidence (information, observations, measurements) that has been used to answer a question e.g. *when prompted can say which of the bubble prints is the biggest* • Ask questions stimulated by their exploration of their world e.g. *How can we make the biggest bubble?*	• Draw on their observations and ideas to offer answers to questions e.g. *Washing up liquid x made the biggest bubbles.* • Respond to suggestions to identify some evidence (in the form of information, observations or measurements) needed to answer a question e.g. *We could measure the bubble pattern to find the biggest bubble.*	• Respond to ideas given to them to answer questions or suggest solutions to problems e.g. *We can measure the bubbles from the different washing up liquid.* • Use straightforward scientific evidence to answer questions, or to support their findings e.g. *You should use washing up liquid x because that made the biggest bubble.*
AF2 Understanding the applications and implications of science	• Identify a link to science in familiar objects or contexts e.g. *The soap turns to bubbles when I blow.* • Recognise scientific and technological developments that help us e.g. *We can get dishes clean by using the washing up liquid.*	• Express personal feelings or opinions about scientific or technological phenomena e.g. *can express positive value of keeping oneself and one's surroundings clean* • Identify scientific or technological phenomena and say whether or not they are helpful e.g. *When the soap makes bubbles in the water it helps get the dishes clean.*	• Link applications to specific characteristics or properties e.g. *The thicker washing-up liquids make different bubbles.* • Identify aspects of our lives, or of the work that people do, which are based on scientific ideas e.g. *understands that scientists are always trying to make better washing up liquids and they constantly test them to learn how to improve them*
AF3 Communicating and collaborating in science	• Present evidence they have collected in simple templates provided for them e.g. *can order the bubble print according to size on a chart given to them* • Use everyday terms to describe simple features or actions of objects, living things or events they observe e.g. *can say which bubble print is biggest*	• Present their ideas and evidence in appropriate ways e.g. *can order the bubble prints according to size and can present results in a table* • Use simple scientific vocabulary to describe their ideas and observations e.g. *can talk about the thickness or runniness of the various bubble mixtures and observe differences in colour, feel etc*	• Present simple scientific data in more than one way, including tables and bar charts e.g. *can present results in a table and bar chart* • Use scientific forms of language when communicating simple scientific ideas, processes or phenomena e.g. *I compared the sizes of bubble prints by measuring them.*

© Pearson Education Ltd 2010. APP for Science Years 1 and 2

Task 14 Lovely Bubbly

Assessment Sheet

	Level 1 Across a range of contexts and practical situations pupils:	Level 2 Across a range of contexts and practical situations pupils:	Level 3 Across a range of contexts and practical situations pupils:
AF4 Using investigative approaches	• Respond to prompts by making some simple suggestions about how to find an answer or make observations e.g. *We could blow gently to make a bubble.* • Use their senses and simple equipment to make observations e.g. *This bubble was biggest.*	• Make some suggestions about how to find things out or how to collect data to answer a question or idea they are investigating e.g. *We could blow bubbles for all of the different liquids and find which is biggest.* • Make measurements using standard and non-standard units as appropriate e.g. *uses multi link cubes to measure diameter of bubble print*	• Identify one or more control variables in investigations from those provided e.g. *can say that they need to use the same amount of liquid each time and blow in the same way* • Make some accurate observations or whole number measurements relevant to questions or ideas under investigation e.g. *can measure diameter of the different bubble prints in centimetres*
AF5 Working critically with evidence	• Respond to prompts to say what happened e.g. *This one is the biggest.* • Say what has changed when observing objects, living things or events e.g. *can say the different mixtures gave different-sized bubbles*	• Say what happened in their experiment or investigation e.g. *can say what they did and what their results were and identify which was the biggest bubble* • Say whether what happened was what they expected, acknowledging any unexpected outcomes e.g. *I thought this liquid would make the biggest bubbles and it did.*	• Describe what they have found out in experiments or investigations, linking cause and effect e.g. *We found that washing up liquid x created the biggest bubble print. We think that this is the best bubble mixture to use for bigger bubbles.* • Identify straightforward patterns in observations or in data presented in various formats, including tables, pie and bar charts e.g. *The thicker liquids made bigger bubbles.*

© Pearson Education Ltd 2010. APP for Science Years 1 and 2

Pearson Education Limited, a company incorporated in England and Wales, having its registered office at Edinburgh Gate, Harlow, Essex, CM20 2JE. Registered company number: 872828

www.pearsonschools.co.uk

Pearson is a registered trademark of Pearson plc

Text © Pearson Education Limited 2010

First published 2010

14 13 12 11

10 9 8 7 6 5 4

British Library Cataloguing in Publication Data

A catalogue record for this book is available from the British Library.

ISBN 978 0 435 03349 1

Copyright notice

All rights reserved. The material in this publication is copyright. Pupil sheets may be freely photocopied for classroom use in the purchasing institution. However, this material is copyright and under no circumstances may copies be offered for sale. If you wish to use the material in any way other than that specified you must apply in writing to the publishers.

Typeset by Mike Brain Graphic Design Limited

Original illustrations © Pearson Education Limited

Illustrated by Andy Cooke

Cover illustration © Clive Goodyer

Printed in the UK by Ashford Colour Press

Acknowledgements

Every effort has been made to contact copyright holders of material reproduced in this book. Any omissions will be rectified in subsequent printings if notice is given to the publishers.

Licence for the use of the APP Primary Assessment Guidelines has been obtained from the Controller of HMSO and the Queen's Printer in Scotland.

Websites

There are links to relevant websites in this book. In order to ensure that the links are up to date, that the links work, and that the sites are not inadvertently linked to sites that could be considered offensive, the links can be accessed at www.pearsonhotlinks.co.uk. Search for APP for Science or ISBN 978 0 435 03349 1.